Author Biographies

Beatrix Potter

Charlotte Guillain

Raintree

D1152167

www.raintreepublishers.co.uk
Visit our website to find out
more information about
Raintree books.

To order:
☎ Phone 0845 6044371
🖨 Fax +44 (0) 1865 312263
✉ Email myorders@raintreepublishers.co.uk

Customers from outside the UK please telephone +44 1865 312262

Raintree is an imprint of Capstone Global Library Limited,
a company incorporated in England and Wales having
its registered office at 7 Pilgrim Street, London, EC4V 6LB –
Registered company number: 6695582

Text © Capstone Global Library Limited 2012
First published in hardback in 2012
First published in paperback in 2013
The moral rights of the proprietor have been asserted.

Edited by Rebecca Rissman, Daniel Nunn,
 and Sian Smith
Designed by Joanna Hinton-Malivoire
Picture research by Tracy Cummins
Originated by Capstone Global Library Ltd
Printed in China

ISBN 978 1 406 23451 0 (hardback)
15 14 13 12 11
10 9 8 7 6 5 4 3 2 1

ISBN 978 1 406 23457 2 (paperback)
16 15 14 13 12
10 9 8 7 6 5 4 3 2 1

British Library Cataloguing in Publication Data
Guillain, Charlotte.
Beatrix Potter. – (Author biographies)
1. Potter, Beatrix, 1866-1943–Pictorial works–   Juvenile
literature. 2. Authors, English–20th century
Biography–Pictorial works–Juvenile literature. 3. Women
authors, English–20th century–Biography–Pictorial works–
Juvenile literature.
 I. Title II. Series
 823.9'12-dc22

Acknowledgements
We would like to thank the following for permission
to reproduce photographs: Alamy Images pp. 5 (©
Urbanzone), 9, 17 right (© Pictorial Press/Photolibrary), 14
(© David Cheshire), 15 (© Pictorial Press Ltd), 20 (© David
Taylor). The Beatrix Potter Society pp. 6, 7 (Rupert Potter);
Corbis pp. 4 (Bettmann/Newspapers), 8 (Rupert
Potter/Time Life Pictures), 10 (Hulton Archive), 17 left
(Andy Crawford), Glow Images pp. 14, 23c (Westend61/
Nobuo Dobhan), The Kobal Collection p. 21 (Weinstein
Company/Rex USA p. 11 (NILS Jorgensen claes), 13 (©
Buhl Gallery), 23a (© Jule Boro), 23a (©
Karel Gallas), 23b (© Petr Foxeta), 23e (© Kevin Eaves),
23f (© vasily), 23g (© Falconia).

Cover photograph of Beatrix Potter pictured outside her
Lake District house near Ambleside reproduced with
permission of Getty Images (Popperfoto). Back cover
image of a rabbit in meadow reproduced with permission
of Shutterstock (wim claes).

Contents

Some words are shown in bold, **like this**. You can find them in the glossary on page 23.

Who was Beatrix Potter?

Beatrix Potter was a writer and **illustrator**.

She wrote and drew the pictures for children's books.

Beatrix Potter wrote many books that we still read today.

Her most famous book is *The Tale of Peter Rabbit*.

Where did she grow up?

Beatrix Potter was born in 1866.

She grew up in London, England.

Beatrix had one brother, who went away to boarding school.

Like many girls at that time, she did not go to school.

What did she do before she was a writer?

Beatrix loved painting when she was a child.

She had lots of pets and liked to draw and paint them.

She also liked to write in a **diary**.

She used a secret code so that nobody else could understand it.

How did she start writing books?

In 1893 Beatrix wrote a story in a letter to a sick boy.

She drew pictures for the story and called it *The Tale of Peter Rabbit*.

Beatrix decided to make the story into a book and **printed** 250 copies.

Then a company **published** the book and she became famous.

What books did she write?

Beatrix wrote many other famous books.

She wrote several stories about rabbits, such as *The Tale of Benjamin Bunny*.

She also wrote *The Tale of Squirrel Nutkin* and *The Tale of Jemima Puddle-Duck*.

Children love to read about her funny animal **characters**.

What did she write about?

Beatrix bought a farm in the Lake District, in Cumbria.

Many of her stories are set in the countryside around her farm.

Many people thought she didn't have a normal life for a woman at that time.

She often wrote about animals that didn't follow the rules, like her.

How did Beatrix draw the pictures in her books?

Some of Beatrix's pictures are black and white.

She drew these pictures using pen and ink, like the artist in the photo.

Other pictures in her books are in colour.

She painted these pictures using paints called **watercolours**.

What else did she like to do?

Beatrix ran several farms in the Lake District.

She raised animals, such as sheep, on her farms.

She looked after nature and animals all her life.

She also loved painting **landscapes** in the countryside.

Why is she famous today?

People still buy Beatrix Potter's books today.

There are many Beatrix Potter gifts and toys.

There are museums and galleries on her life and work.

People have made films about her life and her books, too.

Timeline of Beatrix Potter's life and work

1866	Beatrix Potter was born in London.
1893	She wrote *The Tale of Peter Rabbit*.
1901	She **published** *The Tale of Peter Rabbit*.
1905	She bought Hill Top Farm.
1913	She got married.
1930	Her last book, *The Tale of Little Pig Robinson*, was published.
1943	Beatrix Potter died.

Glossary

 **character** person or animal in a story

 **diary** a book where someone writes down what they have done each day

 **illustrator** person who draws or paints pictures to go with a story

 **landscape** scenery

 **print** make many copies of something, for example a book

 **published** made into a book or put in a magazine and printed

 **watercolour** a type of paint

Find out more

Books

Some of Beatrix Potter's books: *The Tale of Peter Rabbit*, *The Tale of Squirrel Nutkin*, *The Tale of Jemima Puddle-Duck*, *The Tale of Benjamin Bunny*, *The Tale of Pigling Bland*, *The Tale of Mrs Tiggy-Winkle*, *The Tale of Two Bad Mice*, and *The Tale of Tom Kitten*.

Websites

http://www.hop-skip-jump.com/
Visit this website to find out more about Beatrix Potter and the World of Beatrix Potter attraction in the Lake District, Cumbria.

Index